DEDICATION

This story is dedicated to all the people in Albert's life who he loved. Although Albert had a very strict, hard upbringing he wanted to share with everyone the value of being able to show love and receive love from those in his life. He held great respect for his parents and the values they instilled in him to make him into the man he became. Above all, he wanted to share his love story with his beloved wife Rose. Love is forever.

"LOST LOVE & POVERTY"

This is a true story of the life of Albert Gurney. Albert was born on the 12th June 1917 and was the son of Anthony Henry Gurney and Charlotte May Gurney. He was born in Battersea, London. Albert was brought up by his father and stepmother, Eva Violet Gurney.

Albert wanted his family to know about his life and special memories that made him the man he is today. He wrote his story in his ninetieth year, whilst living with his daughter in Epsom, Surrey. Albert died on 20th April 2016, just seven weeks short of his 99th birthday.

Albert had three daughters from his marriage to his beloved wife, Rose. Patricia, born in 1941, and living in Seattle, USA; Pauline, born in 1944, who sadly died in October 1998 and Lilian, born in 1955, with whom Albert had lived with since Rose's death in 1975. He has 12 grandchildren, 26 great-grandchildren and 11 great-great-grandchildren.

This story is Albert's recollection of his memories and his perspective of life and growing up in Battersea.

CONTENTS

Page

"Growing up and early memories"

This is a true story that started for me in 1918. I was one year old when my Dad came home from the 1st World War. He had been fighting in Turkey. His name was Anthony Henry Gurney.

When he arrived home he found my brother, Bob, and myself in one room with hardly any furniture, me in just a vest and possibly no napkin on. He asked my brother Bob (who was 4 years old) where our mother was. Bob said that Mum was over the pub, which was across the road from where we lived. So for possibly a week, we were a family of four, but Dad heard rumours that while he was abroad my Mum was believed to be playing around. My Dad, who had a terrible temper, threw my Mum out, but kept my brother and me Bob with him, so he had to find some place for me to be looked after. He asked his mother to take me in. My mother's name was Charlotte May Gurney.

Life was not what a boy of 18 months old was used to. My grandmother, who was of Romany blood, was not kind to me. When she wanted to go to the pub in the evenings she would lock me in a small cupboard, which was in her bedroom. When she came home, she would let me out of the cupboard and sometimes I had messed or wet myself and many times she called me bad names. I had to put up with this hard and cruel life until my grandmother died in 1920. All the family on my Dad's side came to the funeral and when they came home they were all claiming my grandmother's worldly treasures, trying to settle who was having what.

The next discussion was what to do with me and one after the other of my aunts and uncles said "I will take him", but my Dad's girlfriend, whom I called Mum from the first day I met her and whom I become to love in all the years I was to live with her and my Dad, said they would keep me. She was never cruel to me and I cannot remember her ever smacking me, but as I grew up I could never understand why if she wanted a 1d packet of tea or a loaf of bread, it was always me who was sent to get it, and not my half sisters, Eva or Nina. My stepmother's name was Eva Woodley.

In the 1930's life was hard, and my stepmother was paid 4 shillings and 6d every day by my father to get the food in for each day. He used to pay the rent, which was 10 shillings (now approx 50 pence) and also he used to buy the coal. So every other day Mum would say to me "Albert, go up the Northcote in Battersea and buy from Frosts". Frosts used to sell cheese, butter, also bacon and other groceries. So I would go to the shop and buy 6d worth of bacon bones and when I got home my Mum would sort it out and make bacon stew with the bones. She would save some pieces of bacon for a bacon pudding and some pieces for a bacon sandwich for Sunday breakfast.

At weekends Mum would say "Here Albert, go down Battersea High Street for a flank of beef". She would give me 4 shillings and 6d and I had to go in all weathers, sometimes I would get wet through. When the butcher held a piece of what Mum called a flank of beef and knock the price down to 4 shillings and 6d or 4 shillings, I would shout "I'll have that" and I always made sure I was up the front of the crowd so he could see me and hear me shout out.

There was a bakers which had their depot off of Albert Bridge Road where they sold the stale bread at night time when the drivers with the horses and bakers vans used to come home and then I and the other children would pay 6d for a bag full of stale bread. In those days we used to eat plenty of bread and margarine, except what I called plenty were two thick slices of bread and margarine! It was good bread in those days.

My brother, sisters and myself used to wear second-hand clothes and I always remember when I was 12 years old and I asked my Dad could I have a long pair of trousers like my mates. My Dad was a "totter" (rag and bone man with a horse and cart) and he would get a pair of trousers out of the clothes he had bought that day, cut them down to fit me and sew the bottoms up. He also used to get all my shoes and sometimes they were a size too small for me – sometimes too big! So as you can see we only used to wear second-hand clothes. I used to go out on the rounds with my Dad during my school holidays.

In those days we didn't have washing machines or microwaves. The eldest girl in the family would have to take the washing down to the local washing baths with a small packet of soap powder or buy a large bar of Hudson soap from the attendant for 10d. They would take the washing to the baths in a large bassinet baby pram, in rain or snow. Sometimes they would have to wait up to one hour for a machine to become vacant. If the clothes were really dirty they would have to use a scrubbing board, which would often make their knuckles really, sore. We didn't have any sheets or pillowcases and the bed lice or fleas would be crawling all over your bed. You would be constantly scratching or itching!

In the late 1920's and 30's life was very hard. Money was short and you never had 3 meals a day. I cannot remember ever having breakfast and my parents never let us have school dinners. So we only had one meal a day. I also used to hate Christmas and still do to this day. We never got new bikes or shoes so when I saw my mates with new bikes or a new suit I used to envy them.

In those days you could pay a penny for one cigarette or a penny for a small packet of tea and 2 pennies for one pound of sugar. We never left any of our dinner because if you did, you would never get anything else to eat. People used to get their milk from a man who came round with a horse and cart and you would have to take a jug to him and he would use a container which was either half a pint or one pint and pour it into your jug. From the late 1930's milk was delivered to your door, but we would never leave it outside for long because the young kids would pinch it off your doorstep. You couldn't blame them, because times were so hard on everyone.

I remember some of my neighbours. One in particular would hide behind their curtains when we played with a tennis ball or playing football. When the ball got close to his house he would dash out and grab the ball and we wouldn't get it back. So we would play tricks on him, tying a long bit of string to the door knocker and sit across the street and keep pulling the string which would lift up the door knocker and let it come down and bang the door. He would come out but never suspected any of us, as we would just be sitting across the road. That's how we got our own back on our awkward neighbour!

We also used to play pennies up the line – this was a game where the person who got their penny nearest the line would win. I would love to run errands for the neighbours because you knew that you would get a penny or tuppence. There was one old lady who used to ask me to go to the cat meat shop. On my way back I would eat a slice – it looked like cooked beef and tasted sweet. I have also eaten whale meat, which tasted oily. I am now 89 years of age and when I see in the papers how our youngsters behave today I wonder what the world is coming to. I and many older people like me would have liked to see conscription come back, where young men of 18 years would do 2 years in the army as it would make decent citizens of them. I have always thought that if the Government who took away the powers from parents and teachers hadn't done so, we wouldn't have the problems with the younger elements today and all citizens would have a safe environment to live in.

When I was growing up we used to leave our front door open and neighbours used to chat with each other on their doorsteps. We all knew each other's first name and if someone down our street passed away, there would be a collection down the street to buy a wreath from all the neighbours. But today I don't know the neighbours' names and you never know that someone in your street has died. So you see how life has changed from the 1930's to 2006. I often wish I could choose between 1930 and the 20th century. I would choose 1930, even though it was a struggle to make ends meet. Why is bullying so evident in our schools today? I think that you don't get teachers supervising the children in our playgrounds like they did in the 30's and 40's. Even if you were bullied, you would have a fight with the bully and after the fight you would shake hands and be the best of friends. I am afraid you cannot get into any serious situations today, because bullies are more vicious today than in my day.

Life has changed so dramatically and I cannot see any change in the situation in the coming years. I have often talked to my mates who have moved to the countryside and they all tell me it is a wonderful life living there because you can walk to the pub or shops and walk home without the fear of getting mugged. The air is cleaner than in London and there are many more of the traditional shops like butchers, bakers and greengrocers, who are tending to disappear from the inner cities. You know I envy people who live in villages in the country because they don't know how lucky they are to have a butchers shop, bakers and greengrocers or buy their vegetables or new laid eggs from a farm. Here in London we have to buy them from a supermarket.

I also remember that in my young days if a single girl got pregnant and didn't marry the young man then her parents would throw her out into the streets and disown her. It would be the father of the girl who would make the decision and in those days the father's word was the final word. I often wonder why fathers took these cruel decisions in those days. I could never do that to one of my three daughters as that's when a young girl wants all the love and understanding that their parents could give them, not shun them and turn them away.

If you look at life today it is easier for people to make money. In my early days money was very hard to come by so if we could see a quick way of getting our hands on money we would take risks. We would take the lead off of derelict buildings, sweep snow from outside houses, clean doorsteps or cars for perhaps 12.5p (half crown in those days).

I also used to go over the other side of Clapham Common and set up what was called a 'grotto'. We placed ornaments and old photographs on the ground and placed grass around them making a square for the ornaments to sit in. We would then sit by the grotto and say 'remember the grotto'. People used to give us pennies. If there were any way of making money, we would do it. If we got holes in our shoes we had to place a piece of cardboard inside and hope it would last a long time.

Another trick we had was when a man came around the streets with fruit on a barrow. We would ride beside the barrow on our bikes and have a penknife tied with a bit of string and we would throw the knife at the fruit hoping to stab an apple or a pear. Sometimes you got lucky! We also played spinning the top, which was a piece of wood shaped like a pear with a piece of steel in the bottom. We would wind a piece of cord round the top and spin it on the ground, sometimes spinning onto a penny and if you hit the penny you got to keep it. But I was never any good at spinning the top. We also used to try to get into the cinemas in Battersea for nothing. One of my mates would get money off of his mum and pay to go into the cinema, take his seat and then pretend to go to the toilet. They would then open the back gate of the cinema and let us in. We would drift into the cinema, one at a time, and sit down. We would pick a ticket up from the floor because the attendant would shine their torch and ask for our tickets. We got away with this for a long time but we would sometimes get caught and be thrown out. The only breakfast we got was on a Sunday, and consisted of pieces of bacon (not rashers), fried tomatoes and 1 slice of fried bread.

Our holidays were going down to Kent for hop picking. We went to Days Farm and would go out into the hop gardens from 7 o'clock in the morning till 5 o'clock at night. If you were a pole puller you would be in charge of 7 or 8 bins each with 2-4 pickers on a bin. A farmhand, who was the measurer, would come to your bin and measure out all the hops in a bushel basket and count out aloud how many bushels you had in your bins. A clerk, who we called a bookie, would put the number of bushels in the book and if you wanted a sub (loan from your wages) you would wait outside the farm and the farmer would come out and give you a sub off of your book, which would be deducted at the end of the hop picking season. I remember when we went to the shops in Kent you could smell mothballs, cheese and bacon. I used to like the smell of all these things.

We used to envy the weekend visitors who would come down for the weekend and go back home to London on Sunday night. When hopping season was over our dad would drive the horse and cart with our luggage on it into Tonbridge and buy the boys a new pair of boots for school when we got home. The funny thing was before the last day at the hop fields we always used to say to each other I couldn't wait to get home, but when the last day came we didn't want to leave the hop fields in Kent. I loved going over the Medway with my dog, where we would walk over the fields and walk for miles looking at the wild life. There were rabbits, stoats and moorhens. I would hear the railway engines in the distance, tooting their horns and it was a wonderful sound, sadly not heard anymore. I now look at life and thank God for giving me the pleasures of life I had as a youngster, which sadly youth of today will not have and I wonder would they want to?

I used to sell newspapers in the street on Saturday nights, hollering out "read all about it, baby born in a milk bottle" or "Chelsea's great win" so the more papers you sold the more money you earned. We were paid one penny a quire, so selling 16 papers equalled a quire, so you can see we had to sell a lot of papers.

I also remember that when we went back to school the nurse would come round with a bowl of disinfectant and a steel comb (nit comb). She would run the comb through your hair and if you had nits or fleas you would be sent to the cleaning station and have all your hair cut off. This meant that the girls knew you had fleas because of the close haircut you had. I used to feel sorry for the girls because all their playmates would guess why they had all their hair cut off.

There was always plenty of vermin about – rats, mice, bugs, fleas and lice. You would always go out into the street to play and smell burning clothes where somebody down the street would be burning lice that was in the crutch of their trousers. Even I had to do it to my trousers and they were horrible things. Also nearly all old houses had bugs which used to come through the walls and breed in the wooden springs of the beds and window frames and the only way to get rid of them was to brush paraffin or burn them with a candle.

I used to hate Christmas because on Christmas Day we would hang our sock on the rail of our iron bed and in the morning when we woke up we would empty our sock out and find that we had an orange, a couple of brazil nuts and a new penny. No toys or new clothes. So when I went outside and saw my mates with a new bike or skates I was very envious, and since then I have never liked Christmas because it makes me think about those days. Whilst I might have had some chicken to eat and a warm bed, there were a lot of people around me who had nothing, and some were dying with the cold conditions they were living in.

The title of this story is "Lost Love & Poverty". The reason I called it that is because I never had any love, not from my Dad or my real mother. I would not have known my real mother, who I had never seen for 16 years, if I had passed her in the street. One day my father said to me "Albert, one day your mother will come down the market to see you. If she asks you for money don't give it to her". In those days we used to have a stall in Battersea High Street where my father sold second-hand furniture, clothes, shoes and other goods and you had to wear a badge on your arm to sell goods from the stalls. My father would leave me after the crowds left and leave me there all day. One summer's day I was on my own and standing there looking at me was a woman with a baby in her arms. After a while she said to me "You don't know me, do you?" When I said No, she said I am your mother. There were no tears or cuddles, she just stood there and asked me how I was. I said I was all right, and she said to me "this is your half-brother, Billy". After a while she asked me for 10 shillings, which I gave her. She went straight to the pub in the High Street and when she came out she was drunk, so me and my mate packed the barrow up and took her on a No.12 tram to Lambeth to my other grandmother (my real mother's Mum). It was my misfortune never to see my mother for the rest of my life. I understood from my Mum's sister that my Mum was living with a man and had 3 children by him, all boys.

Today I look back and say to myself "why didn't I grab hold of my Mum and cuddle her with tears in my eyes". Also, why didn't my Mum grab hold of me and cuddle me, and explain why her and my Dad split up. My Dad never, ever explained to me. I only got an explanation from the neighbour who lived downstairs. Neither my aunts on both sides of the family, nor my grandmother on my Mum's side certainly didn't explain, so you see all these years I have only the word of a neighbour.

In the early part of this story I said my father had a bad temper. I and my brother Bob many times in our lives have had bad beatings from my father's whip. If we arrived home late at night, which was say 10.30pm and we should have been home at 10pm, we would climb onto our shed from the street onto the outside toilet, into the kitchen and then to our bedroom and Dad would wait till we were in bed and come into our room and start beating us with his horse whip, sometimes with the thong and sometimes with the butt end which had a ball of gunmetal on the end. We would get out of the bed and crawl under it and my stepmother would come in and ask what all the commotion is about and many times she got a black eye for interfering.

I remember on one occasion he told me to go down the High Street to get some cabbage leaves for our rabbits and I was sitting down playing cards with my mates in the street and my Dad came along and said to me "are you winning?" I replied "a little". Then he said "did you get the cabbage leaves for the rabbits?" I said I had forgotten and he punched and kicked me from where I was playing cards all the way to our house. A few days later my stepmother said to me that I was going to see a gentleman and he would ask me questions about whether my father was ever cruel to me. She said if you say No I will give you 6d. So my stepmother washed me down and put clean clothes on me and my Dad took me to see Inspector Butley, who lived off Lavender Hill in Battersea. We went into a big house. My Dad went into his office and I was called in after. The gentleman asked me questions "did my Dad beat me or kick me?" I said No, he only smacked me on the backside for not doing what he told me to do. So he said get undressed and he looked over my body, I presumed for marks or bruises. He told me to get dressed and when my Dad went back in the Inspector said that if I had been bruised in anyway, my father would have gone to prison for 6 months.

The one thing I hated most in my early life was that when I visited my aunts (they were my Dad's sisters) I would be sad that I had to go home now, as Mum will be waiting to give me my tea. They would say to me "she is not your mother". I would say to them, my Mum brought me up from when I was a baby so I think she is entitled to be called my Mum and I always called her that. Even now, when my children ask me about my stepmother I always say "your grandmother" and I was always proud to call her Mum.

The one thing I missed in my boyhood was to have someone to love me. My Dad never put me on his knee when I cried if I fell over and hurt myself. I used to get a bit of rag and wet it with cold water and dab it clean. There was one time in my life when my Dad and I were at home and my Mum and sisters went away for the weekend. I was in my bedroom on my own and my Dad came in and said to me "come and sleep in my bed", and I can still feel his arms around me every time I think of him. It was like winning the lottery or a pot of gold.

I used to envy my sisters when my Dad or stepmother said to them "come and sit on my knee". Many, many times I have often wished he would say that to me. I could understand that my stepmother didn't say it to me; after all I wasn't her child. That's why I called this story "Lost Love & Poverty".

During my boyhood I was taught by my father that if somebody hurt me I was to hit back or if I couldn't hit them, I was to kick them. Many times at school I got into fights and some I lost, some I won. I was only about '4 foot nothing' at 13 years of age. I used to run a gang of boys and we would go round other neighbourhoods and beat other gangs up, with sticks or poles, broom handles. We thought it was fun in those days and when we had fistfights and it was all over we used to shake hands and become pals.

I remember one fight I had with a boy we used to call Mack. I never did find out his real name but he was the leader of a gang. I was 14 and had left school so I said to my gang that now that I had left school I didn't want to be with the gang any more. This fellow Mack's gang wanted a fight with our gang and they asked me to lead them again. At first I refused, but they kept asking and as the day of the fight grew nearer I said yes. The next day we met the other gang in Culvert Road, Battersea and Mack said it wasn't fair because I was older and had left school. I got into a temper and smacked him one first. I always remembered by Dad's words, "Smack them first!" We fought up and down the road and when I went down nobody pulled him off of me. But if he went down his brother pulled me off of him. In the end, to my relief, he went down and would not get up and they carried him indoors, vomiting all the way to the door.

As kids we used to get up to all sorts of capers. I remember one time at a place called the Latchmere there was a stall, which used to sell rabbits, chicken and fish. Me and a mate would go round the back and pinch the rabbit skins and go to the rag shop and sell them for 3d each and go to the pictures (which was called the Radium Cinema in York Road, or the Super Palace also in York Road, Battersea). Also in Culvert Road there was a derelict site with a wooden garage and we would take the lead off the roofs and sell it to the rag shop. In those days we would do anything in any small way to get money.

A particular incident I remember involved my sister Eva at Latchmere School where we both attended. Somebody came up to me in the playground and told me that the teacher had hit my sister. I rushed into the classroom and threw an inkpot at the teacher and she marched me straight to the Headmaster's office and he gave me six hard strokes of the cane – it didn't half hurt me! I never did any throwing of inkwells again after that.

One lovely memory of my sister, Eva, was when she first met her husband, Tom Williams, in a lane when we were down Kent. This is where we stayed for the night because the farmer wouldn't let us into the field where the hop huts were, so my Dad and Mum, along with myself and my brother and two sisters, pulled onto the grass verge for the night. It was a beautiful September warm night and it seemed that these two young people, who met for the first time, fell in love and I can say that they had many, many happy years together. Sadly, my sister died first, and it seemed that my brother in law died soon after. I always thought in my mind that he died from a broken heart, though he did have that dreaded disease, cancer.

My sister, Nina, met another gypsy boy called Nobby Penfold (his real first name was Frances, but in those days everybody seemed to be called something different from their given first name). They had a wonderful time together until she sadly passed away at a very young age. He never did get married again, and through the years I thought that he would. I know he loved my Nina very much. When she died, she left behind a very young family of 5 children and it seemed that nobody wanted to take them. So my Dad and my stepmother said, "we will bring them up", which they both did. And I can say with pride that they have grown up into a nice close family. In this world I think there should always be family close together, you don't see many families like that today. Thank God, I can see it in my children, with my daughters and me. To me that is as good, or even better, than winning the lottery.

Photo 1: Albert's father - Anthony Henry Gurney

Photo 2: Albert's mother - Charlotte May Gurney

Photo 3: Albert's stepmother - Eva Violet Gurney

"The Army Years"

In 1940 I joined the army. The one thing I missed most was my family. I will always remember the day in June arriving at the barracks in Arborfield, near Reading, and as we got out of the coach, there stood a sergeant with a cane under his arm, barking in a very loud voice "line up here!" And I thought at the time, my God, what have I let myself in for? From then on I knew what discipline was all about. Every day was spent marching on the square, tidying the barrack room up, making sure that everything was neat and making the bed. Equipment on the bed, your boots highly polished (which I had never done in all my young life), but I will say it was the best 6 months that I spent there with my mates who were called up with me in my entire army career.

The worst time was when I went absent without leave for 3 months because I was at home with my wife and children, whom I didn't want to leave. Looking back, I suppose it was because of the discipline, which I wasn't used to. I know my father kept us in check, but you accepted that kind of discipline, but it was hard when it came to somebody else dishing it out. So, when they caught up with me, I will always remember that day. It was on a Monday, which was dustman-calling day. I was out in the back yard with my Dad sorting some rags when the dustman called out. So I said to Dad that I would go and tell them to come through for the dustbin. As I walked up the passage (or as you call it today, the hallway) there standing on the doorstep were two burly policemen who said to me "come along son". I peacefully went to Battersea Police Station with them.

I remember my uncle Bill, he came dashing up the road on his horse and cart and said to them "let him go" and one of the policemen said to him "if you don't hop off you can be put inside with him". It made me smile a bit, but when I got back to the barracks it seemed like a lifetime that I was in Whitehall Detention Holding Unit, run by the Military Police. I was in there for 4 days and slept on thick wooden planks and a blanket. It was freezing in the night and overhead was thick glass that when anybody walked on it, you heard it downstairs in your cell. You had the cell to yourself and it got very lonely. I was glad when the escort came and they happened to be two of my mates, one a corporal and the other a private. The corporal went to put handcuffs on me and I said "leave it out, I won't run away". So the three of us got on a train to Runcorn and I was marched into the Major's office and charged to wait for a Court Martial. I was given 90 days. I went to Chorley Military Prison. They don't treat you with kid gloves in those places. It was "double" or as we called it "running" all the time. We were in big wire cages and when you got up at 6am in the morning you washed and shaved in cold water. You also had to use your razor blade each day, which was taken away from you when you had finished with it.

The stone floors you had to scrub on hands and knees and the food was absolutely horrible. You were given a steel bowl, which when you were first given you had to clean with sand and soap to remove the rust and clean it until your face shone in it. Also, your plate as well. When you got breakfast, which consisted of boiling hot porridge made with water, no sugar or milk, and a mug of cocoa you had to run back to your cage and sit on your bed and when you looked at your plate your bread was covered in cocoa and sloppy. For dinner you had in your bowl boiled rice (no sugar on top), then lamb fatty stew with unwashed carrots, two boiled potatoes in their jackets, and a crust of dry bread. The first and second day I never touched the dinner but after that I couldn't get enough of it. The best meal was at teatime when we got a chunk of cheese and two thick slices of bread and margarine with a cup of tea. You carried the mug of tea in your hand and many times you got hot tea over your hands, but you had to put up with that.

You know when I talk to people about the people of England; I always without a doubt say that Lancashire people were the best that I have ever come across. One day we were being transferred to an open prison to build it and as we were going along in a coach we shouted out to people to give us a cigarette and one kind gentleman gave me all his cigarettes out of his cigarette case. Wherever we pulled up the lads were getting cigarettes thrown in to the coach. I thought that they were great people.

In the prison where we were transferred to the food was very good but was not plentiful. I remember one day queuing for my meal at lunchtime and I was on the end of the queue and when I got to where they were serving (it was shepherd's pie, custard and rice) there wasn't hardly any rice left. I said to the prison guard staff (or sometimes "Sir" as you had to call them), "I haven't got much rice", and he said, "go back and ask for more". This I did and the cook who was on the staff dishing up the meal slapped me across the face as hard as he could. I was seething with pain and anger, but I had to grin and bear it. The screws, as we called them amongst ourselves, were very cruel to the military prisoners.

Another day we had been out digging and it was a hot day so we were sticky and sweaty, so the screws took us to the open showers. We were having our showers and one of the screws asked one poor chap "are you all right?" and the chap said "Yes". Without warning the screw punched him in the stomach and said again "are you all right?" and he said "Yes" again. The screw punched him a second time and said to the poor chap, who was in pain, "next time you say Yes Sir!" I could see by the other screws that they didn't like what they had witnessed.

As I mentioned earlier about the people of Lancashire being good hearted, well the reason I have much praise for them is because they never forgot the prisoners inside the military prison. Each night the screws went down to the pub and the people in the pub would ask the screws how many soldiers were coming out that day. The next morning, people would be waiting outside the prison gates with 20 Woodbine cigarettes and a box of matches for each and every one of us. I can tell you that it was much appreciated. I must say that I never went back again in military prison, but I had quite a few escapes from going back.

One time I came home on leave and my beloved wife gave birth to my darling daughter, Pauline. I was home for 48 hours leave and should have gone back on the Sunday night, but I stayed over until Monday and when I got back my Commanding Officer gave me 14 days field punishment, which was digging large trenches to put the rubbish in. My old sergeant (his name was Fish and we called him Tiddler) said to me "you are taking your time digging those trenches". What he didn't tumble was that I had got one of my mates to put the lorry in front of where I was digging so he couldn't see me taking a breather! I was always trying to dodge duties if I could.

I remember once when we were in Belgium and we were told to sit at the back of our truck with helmets on and not to move, just like you see the German soldiers in war films. So my mate and me were sitting at the back of the truck and Sergeant Major came along and asked me to make him a sandwich. I said to him "sorry Sergeant Major, but I cannot". He said "why not?". I told him that the orders were that we were to obey. He rode off on his motorbike and came back and said to me "forget the order Pat, and make me a cheese sandwich", which I did. He was a good Sergeant Major.

In my early days in the army in 1941-42, we were short of cooks and we were in Runcorn on a gun site. I was always hanging around the cookhouse and worming my way in because it was warm in there and it was snowing and cold outside. One day the officer said to me "why are you always hanging around the cookhouse? Are you interested in cooking?" I said "yes" and he said to the only cook, who was a sergeant, "Do you think that you could learn Gurney to cook in 14 days?". "Yes" he replied, and left me to cook for about 35-45 men. While he was on leave I got rid of all the rations which he had robbed the boys of and I gave them extra portions of cheese, bread, jam, margarine and when he came back he put me on a charge for misusing rations. So the next day I was waiting outside the office and my old Sergeant Major was waiting to march me in and he said to me "so you're in trouble, Gurney?". I tell you I was very scared, I could see detention staring me in the face. He said to me that when I go in and the charge is read out to me, I will be asked if I have anything to say. He said I should say to Sir "how could I misuse rations when there shouldn't have been rations there to misuse?". So I did as I was told and the charge was dismissed. You can see why I have always thought highly of my old Sergeant Major Fish.

As I said earlier in this story I had quite a few narrow escapes. One particular incident sticks in my mind. It happened a week before I went over to France in Normandy. My mates and I were allowed home on leave and once again I went absent and when I went back I was put on close arrest. We were stationed in a park near the docks. We had come all the way from Bognor where we were in billets and from there we travelled to the other side of London. From there we got on the boat to sail to France. I was still on close arrest and while sailing across the sea my Sergeant Major said to me "go in the galley Pat". I said I couldn't because I was on close arrest and shouldn't do any duties, so he went off and came back and said "Gurney, you're now on open arrest". So I ended up in the galley and when we landed in France I was cooking for the lads. I was marched into Major Edward Heath's office and when I told him that my wife and children were bombed out of our house (which was true and my daughter, Pauline, nearly got killed), he didn't believe me and referred me to regiment which meant I would go in front of the Colonel in Charge of the regiment. He said he was sorry but he had to give me 3 days Royal Warrant, which meant I lost 3 days pay.

I went through France to Germany stationed in Hanover and Berlin where I was flown home on compassionate leave. There I was stationed at Aldershot. I was demobbed back into Civvy Street and when I look at my military service it reads as if I was a very bad soldier, but as I look at what I achieved during my service, looking after my comrades and officers while serving with them and had some happy times with all of them. I know if any of them are still alive, and possibly think the same as me. I also thank my comrades whom I served with for 6 years with hope they keep trotting along as I am doing. Good Luck!

I remember while at Aldershot on VE Day. I was put on fire duty while most of the troops went home on weekend leave and the Sergeant Major came up to me and said he was taking me off of fire duty and I was to go to Reading to pick up a prisoner. So I reported to the Guard Room for his release papers and a pair of handcuffs and when I told the Corporal on duty that I was picking up the prisoner at Reading Police Station, they said to me "you'll be lucky – he has got away from escorts two or three occasions previously". So one Private and myself went to the Police Station in Reading to pick up the prisoner. The Sergeant gave me his personal belongings and when he came up from the cells he towered over me. After I signed for his release, I said to him "I won't put the handcuffs on you if you promise me you won't do a bunk". So when we got to Reading, I stuck to him like glue and was relieved when I got him back to the Guard Room and I went on a weekend pass. But I was late back by 24 hours and was put on a Court Martial and got a severe reprimand and 3 days pay stopped. But I was worried that I might go into Detention again because I only had 2 days to go to being demobbed. I often think of my army days and the tricks I got up to.

On one occasion, I came home on a boat and we landed in Hull, so I hung back hoping that I would travel up to London on my own and then when I got to Kings Cross, I would pop over to Victoria Station and get a train to Clapham Junction. So when I saw all the troops going their different ways, I went up to the Officer in Charge and presented my papers and he said to me "where have you been all this time, Corporal Gurney?". I said I had been to the loo so he attached me to another Corporal and 3 soldiers and we all got on a train to London and on the way down I asked whether we were going to stop over in London. He said "No, we will catch a train to Aldershot". When we got to London we had to report to the R.T.O. Office and were told there were no trains tonight, only in the morning. So I said to the Corporal "I am going home". He said to me "what am I going to do?". I said it was up to him. He said what about the 3 soldiers. I said send them to the Union and Jack Club and we would all meet up on Victoria Station. Well, I never went back for 48 hours and when I went to pick up my kit bag at Victoria Station on the Tuesday, they said to me "you're lucky its here because after 24 hours it is taken to Chelsea Barracks". I got on the train to Aldershot and before we got to the station, I altered my papers to say I had arrived Tuesday morning and when I got off the train I couldn't find my ticket. While I was searching my pockets, two Red Caps came up to me and said "what's the matter Corporal?". I said "I have lost my ticket and the Ticket Collector won't let me through". So they said they would take responsibility for me and sent me to the R.T.O. who found me transport to Aldershot Barracks.

The next day I had to stand outside the Adjutant Office and when the Commanding Officer came along, I handed my AB64, which was my pay book, and he said to me "I see you haven't had any leave since last June". I replied "No, Sir". So he told me to report to the Pay Office and get my pay ration card and leave pass. When I got there, I was disappointed because there wasn't an officer there to sign my pass. They told me to come back in the morning, which I did.

When I got home, as I came round the corner to my house, there was my Rose. And the first words she said to me were "what you doing home so soon?". So I said, I'm on leave. She didn't believe me and asked me for my pass and ration book. So I spent 14 days with my lovely wife and 2 children.

Through my Army career I had many sad times. One time I was going to Cornwall with the lads on Gun Practice and just before I left, Sergeant Major came up to me and told me my brother had got killed in a bombing but I had to wait till I got to Cornwall and then they would let me home on leave. When I got to Cornwall, they sent for me at the office and said I would be going home in the morning on the 10am train. Whilst I was in bed, a Sergeant came into the room and told me to report to the office in the morning. When I got there, my Adjutant told me I would not be going because it was only my sister-in-law and 2 nieces who had been killed, but if it had been my brother I would get a 14 day pass to go home. What silly rules the army had in those war years.

Another sad occasion was when we were in an apple orchard and word came back to us that one gun emplacement had been hit by a shell and one officer and one of my old mates called Crocker, who came from Norwich, had been killed outright. That's when war became serious for me. And another chap called Chamberlain came back from behind the front lines and was in a terrible shock, he tried to hide under the jeep seat. I never saw him again.

One of the worst things I had to do was to shoot a puppy, which I had become quite attached to. I used to have him sleep on my bed, which was in a lean-to. It was a very small place that we made up of corrugated iron and my bed was on compo boxes, or as you would say, food boxes. We had our kitchen in a small area of the lean-to and inside we had a petrol driven cooker and oven. It was very cold outside, with about 2 feet of snow, and somehow the puppy had got into the bottom of the oven. We didn't know he was there and I put the pots of water on for 10.30am tea break. He must have been under the oven for a good ten minutes. I heard him squealing out in pain. I went outside to look for him, came back into the kitchen, and my mate John said the puppy was under the oven. We pulled the burner out and the puppy ran across the field. I never saw him for about a week. He came back and was in a sorry state. He was blind and his mouth was festered and he was very weak. My mate said, "Pat, you will have to put him down". So I took him into the forest, tied him to a tree and shot him dead. I buried him in the forest. It was one of my saddest days losing that loveable pup.

From my days at school until I joined the Army in 1940 my life has been very hard. I sometimes wish that I had been born in the 1950's or 60's because in my days I had to work for peanuts for 7 days a week. I used to get up in the morning at 6am, go down to the stables in Culvert Road Arches, put the harness on the horse, and harness the horse to the cart. I would then go back round home and wash in the water my Dad had washed in because it was warm, otherwise I would have had to wash in cold water. Then I would have a cup of tea and drive the horse to Chiswick, Wormwood Scrubs, Shepherds Bush or Acton. We would put cards in the doors of the houses and then call back if they had anything to sell. I worked 7 days a week, sometimes till 8 o'clock at night and was paid 10p per week right up to the age of 23 years old.

I well remember my brother, Bob, coming home on a Saturday night with the day's takings and counting the money out, and putting 10 shillings in his pocket and I was very angry that he did that. But when I took over the stall I did the same, so I understood why my brother robbed my father, because my father didn't pay us enough pocket money and it led me to be dishonest.

Photo 4: Albert - In uniform

Photo 5: With Army Comrades

Photo 6: In the Army kitchen

"Hop picking"

Every year we used to go hop-picking in Kent. At the age of 8 years old my father would give me a tub to pick the hops in and said when I picked 8 tubs full I could go and play. My sisters weren't allowed to pick hops so they could play all the time and if I was to slow down and look around my Dad would swipe me with a piece of hop vine. It used to hurt me terribly, so I would pick hops as quick as I could and people used to throw me pennies because I became very good at it.

My sisters, Eva and Nina, were always fighting and rowing over something or other. One day, they caught a big bull frog and Eva said "its mine, Nina, I found the frog – its mine". They both got hold of the frog's legs and pulled it apart and both ended up in tears. My sister Eva had a vile temper, just like my father. She didn't suffer any fools! But my sister Nina was a little angel, very loving and inoffensive. I missed her very much when she died of leukaemia. My late daughter, Pauline, always reminded me of my Nina, as she had the same loving ways and a heart of gold. I remember one day we were coming home to London from Kent and Nina was cuddling our dog, Nell, on the back of the cart. The dog jumped off the back and nearly got run over and I could see the look of fear on my sister Nina's face, and to this day I often wondered whether the shock of that incident led to my sister getting that terrible illness, which took her life at the age of 27 years old.

One year we were coming home from Kent, and I was driving a beautiful mare called "Kitty". When we got into Bromley, an RSPCA Inspector pulled me in and told me to take the horse and cart down a side street. I was 17 years of age. I asked why he had pulled me up and he said that someone had phoned them and said that I had been cruel to the horse. I told him that I don't carry a whip. The horse was covered in white sweat and I told him that the horse had been turned out in a field and would be like that from eating grass and it was a hot day. He told me to take the horse out of the cart and take the harness off of the horse, which I did. He was looking for whip marks but to my relief there were none. How could there be when I didn't carry a whip and knew that I would not hurt my horse? What I was most concerned about was whether the collar of the harness had rubbed any part of the horse. The Inspector said to me "Son, don't put the mare back in the cart – she's too good a horse for a cart". So he got me to put the cart in a coalman's yard and when I got to where my Dad was waiting with my Mum and sisters and all our belongings on the other cart, I explained what had happened to my father. He said I would have to ride the horse home bare back (no saddle) and when I got home (which was 11 o'clock at night); there was some cold fish and chips on the table for me.

Life was extremely hard between 1930 and 1940. One incident I still think about to this day. We were down Kent hop-picking and my sister Eva threw a stone at me and I asked her to stop. But she kept on throwing the stones at me, so I threw one back at her and it hurt her on the knee. She screamed and screamed, which got the attention of my father, who was carrying a big pole with a hook on the end which was used to cut the hop vines off the wire above. My sister told my Dad that I had thrown a stone at her, but didn't tell him that she had thrown one at me. So he came charging at me as if he was a soldier in the war. All the people around, mostly women, screamed. I managed to dodge the hook and then ran down the field till my father had cooled down. It was the fright of my life and can remember that it was in the summer of 1933 when I was 17 years of age.

In the early part of this story I mentioned that I used to take the dog across the Medway. Well, one day when my daughter was 11 years of age, I took her across the Medway. As we got to a pond in the woods I said I will show you a moorhen on a nest in the middle of the pond. Sure enough, there was the nest with a moorhen sitting on her eggs. Then, 11 years later, my other daughter, Lilian, was 8 years old and we went with my wife and a cousin, across the Medway. I said to my daughter, come for a walk and I will show you a moorhen on a nest in the middle of the lake. I felt a bit doubtful because of the years that I had been away from the Medway, but my fears were not confirmed because there in the middle of a pond was the nest with a moorhen sitting on it. It obviously wasn't the same moorhen, but it just goes to show you if people left wildlife alone, they would still be there today – hares, foxes, rabbits, pheasants, partridges and many other birds.

"Epsom Racecourse- and memories of my Father"

In my early childhood, we used to go to Epsom to get a living on the racecourse. You could hear the skylarks in full song singing in the sky all day but sadly today you would be lucky if you heard one signing at all. We would go to Epsom from Battersea, which was about 15 miles, and we would camp on the Downs. My father would put up four poles with tarpaulin around and dig a big hole and I and my brother Bob would have one each and shout out "Accommodation!". Men would give us an old penny or sometimes six pence in old money and at the end of the day we would give him all the money. In the evenings, me and my cousins would ride bareback over to the water trough so the horses had a drink and we would race each other. That to me was the best part of the day.

One of our trips to Epsom was for the 3 day meeting, and it rained heavily all day. Myself and my sisters and brother sat in the tent eating sherbet, and my father pulled cars out of the mud with his horse and got paid 10 shillings for every car he pulled out. My ambition in life was to become a jockey. Many times, my father was told "why don't you let Albert go to the stables in Epsom and be a jockey". If I had been able to go I would possibly have gone to the late Stanley Wootton, who used to have quite a lot of youngsters training as stable lads and hoping later to become jockeys. But my father would not agree to this as I had to work for him. I worked for him until 1940 when I was called up for military service, but looking back I don't regret that I didn't become a jockey because I possibly wouldn't have met my lovely Rose and had three wonderful daughters, whom I love with all my heart.

My Dad wasn't all bad. He had some good points as well as the bad ones. I remember when I was eight years old and many times my Dad would take me fishing. I can remember it as if it were yesterday. We used to go to Windsor and get on a little boat called the Rabbit and it used to chug up the Thames to a lock which was called Bovenly Lock and run by a lock keeper called Mr King. Dad had a punt there and from the lock we would go back towards Windsor and drop anchor and start fishing. It was great fun especially when we got on shore and made a fire to have a cup of tea. The tea tasted absolutely marvellous. I always say that a mug of tea made from water boiled on an open fire is the best cup of tea you will ever taste. Early one Sunday morning we were moving down the river to a fishing spot and I was sitting on a wooden chair when all of a sudden we went under a willow tree. A thick branch whisked me off the chair into the river and at the time I was eating a bar of chocolate. The other man in the boat pulled me out by my legs, which was all that was showing in the water, saving my life. My Dad took me to the shore and built a big fire and took my clothes off and gave me his overcoat and dried my clothes for me.

I used to like going fishing with my Dad. He always played jokes on his mates. One was called Dodger and another one was called Tubby. I remember one early morning in September while we were all asleep. My Dad would get a breast of lamb and put it on his mates fishing line and sling it in the river and wait till we got up. One of his mates would say he's got a bite, because his fishing would be out all night in the river with possibly a worm on the line or a small dead fish called a gudgeon. They would think that because the line had sunk (from the weight of the breast of lamb) that they had caught a big fish! My Dad would get a big laugh out of his pranks. Also, his mates would do the same to him. We also went fishing in Sunnymede. I always enjoyed going there to fish.

But my great love is Kent. I used to roam all over the Medway and I and my dog, Nell, would roam for miles through field after field, seeing wild rabbits, hear the birds singing such as chaffinches, linnets, goldfinches and wild pigeons cooing in the trees. It was the best part of my boyhood.

Once when I was walking back home through the fields, it started raining a warm fine rain. All of a sudden, a stoat jumped up in the air trying to catch a goldfinch which was flying just above the tall grass. But to my joy it missed – it was nature in the raw. Sometimes I would go and pick mushrooms which grew wild under an oak tree, close to the trunk of the tree. Some of my cousins used to ask me where I found them, but I would never tell them because if I did they would pick them all and I wouldn't find them there anymore. They would go there before me and take them.

I used to go down to the woods with my Dad and my uncles with a ferret called Charley. We would find four or five rabbit holes and put nets over each hole, peg the nets down and when my Dad put the ferret down we would wait. Then suddenly, we would hear a sound like thunder coming from below the ground. We had to get ready because as the rabbits came rushing up the hole we would grab them. Dad would kill them and then Mum would make a rabbit stew for us all.

What I liked most was when we went hop picking. My Dad would say to me "Albert, I want you to put the mare in harness and take Mum to Tonbridge to get the shopping". I always enjoyed going with Mum because she would give me a half-crown while she went shopping. I would leave the horse outside the café with her feed while I had my breakfast. Then I would go and meet Mum and carry her shopping back to the horse and cart and head back to the farm. Sometimes I would get back later and it would be too late to go out to the hop fields to pick hops because the bailiff would blow his whistle. You knew then that you didn't have to pick any more hops until Monday. Sometimes picking hops was not very nice. You would get pollen on your hands and when you had a sandwich for lunch, the pollen would get onto your sandwich and into your mouth and it tasted like bitter alum, a very nasty taste. And you never seemed to enjoy your sandwich. Some people, like my brother Bob, used to put a bit of newspaper round the sandwich so they never got any pollen on it.

When hopping was all over, we used to drive into Tonbridge and my Dad would buy me and my brother Bob a pair of boots and my sisters each a pair of girl's shoes and that's all we got for picking hops for a month or 6 weeks and never got any pocket money. You would be envious when other children would say that their Mum was going to give them 10 shillings (50p) to go to the pictures when they got home. Myself and my brother didn't think it was fair and that's what it was like in the early 30s.

One time I was working at the father's stall in the High Street and he said to me that when I took the barrow home he wanted me to fetch 2 half-hundred weights down to Windsor for him on the back of my bike. Dad was a very keen fisherman. So on the Saturday night, me and my mates went on the road towards Windsor and got as far as Slough and camped there for the night. I unloaded my bike, putting the weights onto the ground. When we woke up and had our breakfast, we go on the road to Windsor and when we got to the riverbank the first thing my father asked me was "where are the weights?". I said I had forgotten them. He made me go all the way back to Slough to get them on my own because none of my mates would go with me. I couldn't blame them for not going back all that way, could I?

"Meeting my Rose - the love of my life"

When I used to think back through my life, I said that if I ever get married and have children they would have all the loving I could give them and I think up to the present day I have achieved that aim. I met my wife, Rose, in a pub called the British Flag in Culvert Road, Battersea. I was in uniform. I went into the pub with my stepmother and a young lady was dancing with one of the stepbrothers and I thought she was a married woman. Whilst sitting at the table, I was looking at my sister-in-law and saw the anger on her face because her husband, my stepbrother, was dancing with this young lady. So I got up and went over to them and said "can I cut in?". While I was dancing with her I was chatting to her and asked her if she was married. She said she was not and when the dance finished she asked whether I could like to meet her grandparents. "Yes" I said. We went over to her grandparents and I shook hands with them and asked if they would like a drink. Her grandmother said she would like a Guinness and the grandfather wanted a pint of ale. When I went up to the bar and brought the drinks back to them someone pushed me forward and the drinks went all over the grandmother's clean white apron! She called me all the names she could remember! I thought to myself, that's put the block on making a date with the young lady.

I was beginning to think it had put a block there for me because I asked her for a date to take her to the pictures (cinema) and she made excuses about doing the ironing on Monday. So I said, what about Wednesday? She said I wash my hair that night. So I said forget it. I had the feeling that somehow I had blown it. But then the opportunity came up again. I was going to see my Dad down the market, as I was home on leave for 14 days. As I was walking up my street I saw this young lady friend, Winnie, whom I knew very well. As we were talking Winnie asked me was I going to the pub that night. I said I was and I would see her up there, but I ignored the other young lady, whom I knew as Rose.

That night I went into the pub, hoping upon hope that Rose would be there and to my joy she was! But another evening, I went to her grandmother's house (off Battersea High Street) to take her out. When I knocked on the door her grandfather came down and handed me a letter and said Rose didn't want to see me anymore. As I walked away from her house reading the letter (which said "Sorry Albert, I have gone back to my old boyfriend"), I said to myself "well, there's plenty more fish in the sea". I began to think were there any more for me? And the doubt of many years ago came back to haunt me.

But my fortune seemed to change for the better when I came home on leave for 7 days and went down to Kent where my parents were hop picking. I met another girl called Rose who came from Islington and we got on like a house on fire. But it was only a hop picking romance which ended when we all finished the hopping season. I was going to see a cousin of mine and there in her house was a beautiful gypsy girl. Yes, it was another girl called Rose! It seems that the name Rose will not go out of my life.

I was with Rose from Mitcham for possibly 3 months but sadly it came to a sad end once again. I went over to Mitcham to take her out and her brother said to me that he didn't want his sister going out with me anymore. So once again I began to think perhaps I was unlucky with girls. But as time went by I started to forget girls and started to go out with my mates and play cards in one of their houses all night. I also started to go round the fair, which was up Clapham Junction, and enjoy myself on the dodgems and throwing at skittles for packets of cigarettes. You know, I didn't start smoking until I was 19 years old. My Dad saw me with a cigarette and said "I see you are smoking?". Defiantly, I replied that Yes I was. I will always remember his words – he said "you will be sorry". My Dad was a wise old man. Often he would ask me why I hadn't gone totting on a particular day and would say to me "you know, lad, if you go out to work you will earn a Pound but if you stay at home you will spend a Pound". And when I look back to what he said to me, he was right. Something else he told me was to look after my customers and my customers would look after me. I found that this was also true.

Well, it seemed that life was going to be very difficult for me to find a young lady who one day would be my wife and I was beginning to believe that it would never happen. But it did and now I will tell you all about it.

It was July 1940. I was in the pub and whilst playing darts in walked Winnie and she had Rose with her. We got talking again and started going out together again. It lasted for 3 weeks and we had a row. I don't know whose fault it was, but let's say it was my fault. Well, we went on our different ways again and I started to go back to the fair once again. I possibly thought that perhaps I would find another young lady but it wasn't to be. One Saturday night my cousin, Letty, came up to me and said that some boy had taken Rose down an alleyway. So I ran down the alleyway and told the guy to lay off of my girl or I would beat him up. I took her by the arm and took her back to the fair. She said she wanted to go to the pub to her friends so I said I was taking her home and if she didn't come I would sling her handbag over the wall. She started to cry and said to me "I will tell my Gran", so I said to her that I would tell her Gran what had happened. So we started to go out together once again and through that year she told me about her life and what she went through. And I thought my life was hard.

She told me that she and her sister and two brothers were taken away from their mother and put in a convent. While she was there she told me life was very hard. She went into service in Green Street, Kent and one day her grandfather came and took the two girls away from the convent but left her brothers there. If her grandfather had not rescued them, they would probably have become Nuns. She only had two weeks to become a Novice to be prepared to become a Nun. So you see, I was not the only one who had a hard life.

One evening, whilst we were talking about hard times, she told me that her mother and stepfather were so poor that they had a meal called kettle broth. This consisted of dry bread, a little salt and pepper and hot water poured over it. And that's what they had to eat. The 1930s were extremely hard for many people.

When I courted Rose, whom I loved and still love today, I was getting 5 shillings per week from my Dad. It was very hard to get 5 shillings out of my Dad. Dad and I used to save iron bedsteads, old bike frames and other light iron and Dad would say to me "Albert, take the iron out of the garden up to the railway yard in Wandsworth Road". I used to get 15 shillings or one Pound for it. But that meant I would get wages for that week.

Well, now I will get back to what happened to my darling Rose and me. We were courting for about 3 months and I asked her to marry me. After about 10 minutes, which to me seemed like a lifetime, she finally said Yes. So I applied for special leave and we got married on 30 November 1940.

Our first child was born in September 1941 and was called Patricia. Thereafter, everybody that I served with in the army called me Pat. So for the 6 years that I was in the army, I answered to the name of Pat. After 6 months in the army I was placed in army prison for 90 days for overstaying my leave. When I got out of detention I applied for compassionate leave to be with my wife and child. When I got home my wife was round my mother-in-law's house with the baby, whom I had never seen. When I walked in my wife said after a while "Well, don't you want to see you daughter?". I went over and went to pick up one of the two babies that were lying there and as I did so, my wife said "No, not that one, the other one!". The one she pointed out was completely bald and I felt a bit disappointed because she had no hair and the other baby (who became my daughter's auntie because she was in fact my mother-in-law's baby) had a lovely head of hair.

Three years later in May 1944, our darling daughter Pauline was born, who had beautiful auburn hair. It wasn't until 11 years later in September 1955, that our other darling daughter, Lilian, was born. Over the years, Lilian has become a little mother to me, looking after me for the last 32 years since losing my beloved Rose, who died in 1975 following a stroke. And for those 32 years I have missed her and sometimes cry when I think of her. Every night I say, "Goodnight and God Bless you Darling". I try not to miss saying Goodnight Darling if I can. Sadly, in October 1998, my darling Pauline passed away and I miss her very much. I feel that I have let my Darling wife down because as she lay dying I promised her that I would take care of our sweet darling daughters and now one of my jewels in the crown, as I have called them, has passed away from cancer. So it only leaves me with my two precious jewels but I am afraid the crown has no meaning anymore. But my two jewels have become more precious to me now than life. My one wish if I was allowed one would be to God – "Why didn't you take me instead of my sweet Darling Rose?".

You know all my married life I always had doubts that my Rose loved me. I suppose it was because growing up without love put these doubts in my mind. But I was to be proved wrong. One day I became ill after falling off my bike and injuring my shoulder. My Rose phoned for the doctor and when he came he said I had to go straight to hospital. I had to wait for the ambulance and as I walked towards the ambulance to get in I looked back towards where my wife was standing in the doorway and I could see tears in her eyes. So then all the doubts that I had had for the last 37 years was no more and I knew from then on that she loved me for all our happy times and love together. I must Thank God for giving me 37 happy loving years and also my Rose for giving me three precious and loving daughters. Also, thanks to all their children and my grandchildren and great-grandchildren and great-great-grandchildren whom I love dearly.

I Love You, Rose
I Love You, Pauline
Also You, Lilian
And My Patricia

God Bless you all and I hope that you, Lilian and Pat, have a longer loving life than I did.

Love Dad
xxxxxxx

Photo 7 - Albert and his Rose

Photo 8: Albert with Rose and daughters Patricia and Pauline

Photo 9: Patricia and Pauline

Photo 10 : Lilian

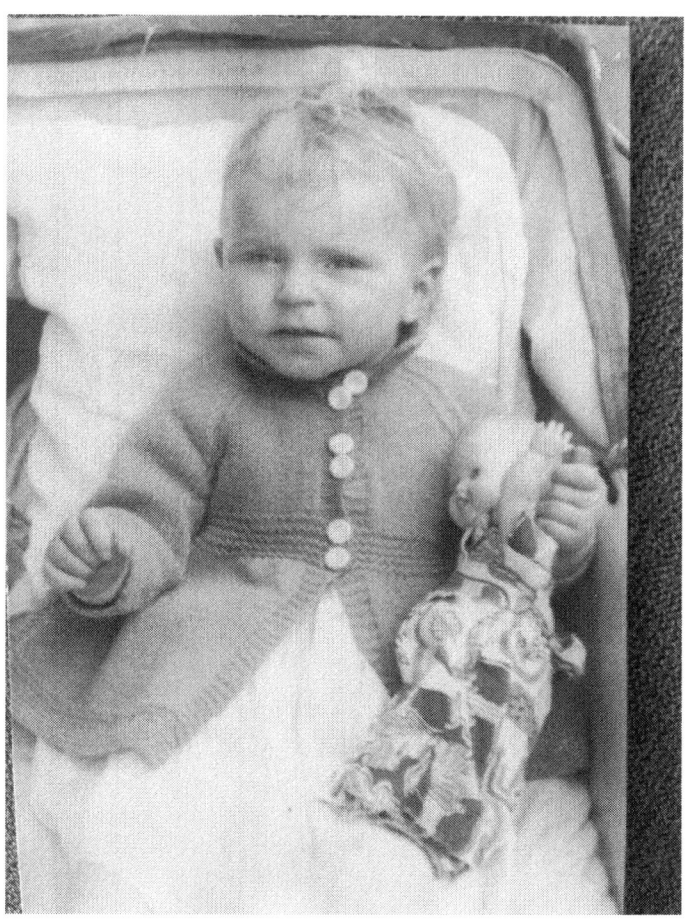

Photo 11: Family - Albert's world

Photo 12: Albert with his horse Tom and Lilian

Epilogue - by daughter Lilian

I feel it is correct that I write this epilogue now that my Dad, Albert, has passed away and is unable to write it himself.

I was an unplanned baby, born 11 years after my sister Pauline. Both Mum and Dad really wanted a son after having two girls. And for a fleeting moment following my birth in St Teresa's Hospital in Wimbledon they thought they have a son as the Nuns' attending the delivery announced "you have a little lasorroo" as the cord was wound around my neck. Dad told me that his disappointment soon changed to happiness once he saw me and realised that he had yet another daughter.

My memories of early childhood are of an extremely loving family life, surrounded by aunts, uncles, cousins and of course my sisters and my Mum and Dad. We felt very loved even though we were considered a poor family. My Mum always worked, doing housekeeping and later as a cleaner. In fact she worked for the famous Shirley Bassey and I have fond memories of sitting in Shirley's kitchen eating breakfast with her children whilst Mum busily cleaned around her house.

Dad was a "totter" or rag and bone man. He worked 6 days a week, rising at 5am so that he could tack up the horse and cart at the stables in Culvert Road (Mills Yard) and he would then travel all the way over to Shepherds Bush - he called it "The Round of Mars". He was very respected by most of his customers - he retold stories to us of some awkward folk who would throw his calling card in the bin (these cost money to be printed and Dad always collected them at the end of his rounds when he would knock on doors and ask whether they had any rags for him or he would politely ask for his card back). He told us of one man who said "No, I've chucked it in the bin" and Dad said "Well that wasn't very clever was it Sir". But on the whole he loved his customers and had very good relationships with them. They trusted him and looked forward to his visits as he would pay them for the rags and other goods they gave to him.

When Dad packed up the totting as business was falling and he wasn't earning enough, he found a job working as a cleaner at the American Embassy in London. He loved this job, going about his work every day with his friendly smile, polite manners and keen enthusiasm to get his areas clean and sparkling. One of his most exciting memories is of being asked to clean the gold eagle on top on the building. Dad could not resist climbing on and sitting astride it, admiring the views across London, before he climbed down and gave it a good clean! He felt quite proud that he is probably one of the only people to have done this.

For a while during this time we had an opportunity to move to Southampton. My Mum was a housekeeper for a very rich family in Cheyne Walk, Chelsea and the lady she worked for asked whether she would like to move to Southampton as her housekeeper with my Dad as the Cook and general handyman. So around 1965 we moved to Southampton to live in a cottage tied to the mansion house, leaving my sister and her husband and son Albie to live in our house in Oulton Street. This proved to be a wonderful opportunity for both my parents as my Mum was in her element housekeeping for the family and my Dad was so happy to be in the kitchen cooking delicious meals for them. Very soon he was cooking for dinner parties and gatherings where some very famous people attended, including Lord Montagu of Beaulieu - his food was loved and people were soon asking whether he could come and cook for them! Not bad for a poor Battersea boy!

I had a wonderful time before I had to attend my new school as Dad would come home frequently with abandoned or injured animals - a squirrel, a pigeon, a rabbit and even a baby seagull. I was in my element taking care of them until they could be released back to the wild, taking serious attention to the advice Dad would give me about how to handle and feed them. He really was a font of all knowledge and his understanding of wildlife was fantastic. There wasn't much he didn't know, often telling me of the mating seasons, what type of bird we might see, where they might make their nests and all sorts of other wonderful nature facts. The fields around the estate always produced casualties of small animals or birds when they did the harvesting so these always kept us busy trying to help them recover and survive. He also took care of the family's chicken coop and he loved choosing the hens, making their coop and then taking me with him every day to check for eggs.

Regretfully, I was unable to settle in Southampton and knowing that I was unhappy my parents told the family that we would be going home to Battersea. The lady of the house offered many options to help us stay: for me to have my own pony, to include me with parties and events with her own children, for my Dad to learn to drive and he would be able to drive me to school and collect me instead of our 3 mile walk. But my parents had already made their decision to return to where I would be happy again. My Dad stayed on at the property for a further 5 months on his own until the family were able to recruit replacements as he did not want to let them down. The family gave him a glowing reference and were very sad to lose both he and my Mum.

When we were all finally back living in Battersea my Dad took a job working for a major catering firm. He worked long, hard hours and the work was very physical. My Dad was only 5' 1" tall but he certainly had the strength and ability of men much bigger than him and he worked solidly and was soon one of the best workers the company had. Life at this time was going well as both my parents were working and the money situation was easier for them again

Dad's final job before he retired at the age of 65 was as a messenger/porter at the Ministry of Agriculture, Fisheries and Food in Whitehall. He absolutely loved this job and went to work happy and smiling every day. He just loved meeting and helping people and he quickly became Senior Porter, a role which he took very seriously. When it was time for him to retire he did not want to - he wanted to carry on working as long as possible. He had a fabulous retirement party where he thoroughly enjoyed hearing everyone's thoughts and views on him - they all said the same: he was reliable, trustworthy, honest and extremely hard working. He felt very proud that people had this view of him - after all he had been striving all his life for people to like and respect him.

In the years between my Mum having her first stroke in 1971 until her death in 1975, my Dad's own health started to suffer. Because he was so worried about his beloved Rose he started to lose weight, couldn't sleep well and was constantly stressing about her and her care. When she died, he weighed just 7 stone and looked like he had come out of a concentration camp. We all rallied around him, taking care of him, feeding him and encouraging him to return to work so that he had a purpose in life again. It was an extremely sad time for both him and our family.

My childhood was extremely happy. Every day I would listen for my Dad to come home, whistling his heart out as he walked down the street. When he came in I always got a hug and a kiss and I would sit with him whilst he had a hot cup of tea, listening to his tales of how his day had been, how Tom his horse was and whether he had earned enough money. I remember that every single night he would read me a story in bed - it always had to be about a black stallion and I would not go to sleep until he had told me the whole story, which he would change slightly each night to add some more excitement for me. This was obviously what fostered my love of horses!

When my Mum died on 12th November 1975 our world collapsed. I had just had my first child, Lisa, on the 10th October and I can remember coming home from St Thomas' Hospital back to my Mum and Dad's house in Freedom Street. Our GP was there and he asked to see myself and my Dad in another room. He then told us that my Mum was going to die as she had developed gangrene in her foot and only surgery would save her - however, it was possible that she would not survive the surgery as she had already had 3 major strokes. We decided to keep her at home and for the next few weeks we nursed her and cared for her so that we could be with her every moment of every day.

Life was heartbreaking following her death as after the funeral my sister Pauline and myself would go to Dad's house each day, both with a newly born baby, to tidy up, build a fire in the fireplace and cook him a dinner. When he would come home from work he would look so forlorn and empty. He told me much later that when we left him each evening at around 5.30 so that we could go home to our husbands and cook them dinner he would bolt all the doors and sit by the fire thinking to himself how could he end it all and be with his beloved Rose again.

So Albert came to live with myself and my husband as we gave up both properties and were given a council house in Linstead Way, Wandsworth where we lived as one family unit. Two more children followed, Jamie in 1977 and Laura in 1980. Dad had found a purpose again and he loved living as a part of a family again. My sister Pauline lived in Roehampton so we were able to visit every week and she would visit our house too along with her children Albie, Karen, Jason and Rosina. We visited Pauline and her family every Sunday and every Wednesday she would visit Dad and they would go off to Harrington's Pie and Mash shop in Selkirk Road, Tooting for their weekly dose of pie and mash. Dad always had eels with his and it was one of his favourite foods.

Whilst we were keeping Dad busy with our children in the UK, my sister Patricia who had lived in Seattle USA since 1958 also produced 5 more grandchildren for him: Patricia, Susan, Peter, Marti and Maria. Dad visited them often, sometimes each year, from around 1977 right up until he was in his mid nineties, travelling on his own on the long transatlantic flight. He was deeply loved by both families each side of the ocean, instilling his zest for life, showing us how to love and respect and telling all who would listen of his life memories. He thought it was important that all the children knew their family history, particularly the Romany side and he was immensely proud of his parents and their work ethics. This was something that he instilled in all of us, always happy to help us with any difficulties we were facing and encouraging us to face them in the best way possible and work towards solutions.

Following Albert's retirement he found a new role in life - he took on the role of taking my three small children to school and nursery each day, helping them to get ready in the mornings and then picking them up at the end of each school day. My children have fond memories of their daily routine. I would go to work and Dad would organise them for school. This consisted of him preparing them their breakfast, letting them wash their face and hands with a bowl of warm water in front of the fire in the living room (not a practice I would have encouraged but I only found out when they were adults!) and making sure they were dressed spick and span ready for their day at school. Off he would go with them, two dogs in tow, telling them all about the birds they would see and seeing each of them into their respective classrooms. Then at the end of their school day he would pick them up, with whatever sweets they had asked for in the morning and they would make the journey back home again. He was a well liked figure in the playgrounds with parents and children alike bidding him good morning and usually resulting with him offering other children a sweet from his pocket!

Albert also was a regular figure in the school classroom. Teachers would ask for him to come in and cook with the children and he would patiently talk them through the process of what they were going to cook, helping them to mix recipes and recalling to them his memories of the food he used to eat as a child which was vastly different to what these children were used to. He also made a few visits to talk to classes of children about his service in the war. He felt it was important that children knew the history of World War II and understood the devastation and hardship it caused but also the commitment and bravery of all who served. All of Albert's visits were eagerly accepted by staff and children and he absolutely loved doing it.

In 1997 our world fell apart when my sister Pauline became ill and after many tests and hospital appointments was diagnosed with lung cancer. Pauline started her treatment and we were all in awe of her as she battled cancer, taking every treatment in her stride, always with a smile on her face as she was determined to beat this dreadful disease. As the months went on Pauline started to have other areas where the cancer had spread and she finally succumbed to the disease on the 26th October 1998. Dad's world fell apart again - I can still see his face one night when I returned from visiting Pauline in hospital after I had finished work and he immediately asked me how she was doing. I decided to tell him the truth "I'm sorry Daddy but we are going to lose our Paula". These words crushed him but I knew that he had to face the fact that she would not be able to beat the cancer. My Dad always said after losing Paula that unless someone has lost a child they would never know or imagine how he felt. He never really got over her death and our only blessing was that she was buried right next to my Mum's grave so he could still visit her whenever we went to the cemetary. Life was never the same for us or her lovely family.

Albert remained very fit and active throughout his life apart from blood pressure and some damage to arteries in his legs. As each milestone was reached - his 70th, 80th and 90th he held the same philosophy in life. He always tried to do things he probably shouldn't have - jumping on trampolines in Seattle with his grandchildren, riding a BMX bike he found in the street when we moved to Stoneleigh in 1999 (aged 82!), and climbing up a ladder and through a bathroom window for a neighbour when he was 84 where he fell into the bath smashing his head open. This was to be the start of the many falls and accidents he would suffer from that time. He probably had many more that he did not tell me about as he would not have wanted to worry me even more.

Whenever Dad had a fall I would come home from home and find him covered in blood, with either a towel or bandage covering the cuts he had received. I would immediately ask him "why didn't you call me at work". He would reply "I'm OK, it's only a little cut". He would often refuse to go to hospital saying he didn't want to make a fuss. In hindsight, I now realise that I should have insisted as they would probably have found some of the bleeds on his brain which later developed into more serious conditions.

It was also around this time that Dad's skin became very fragile and whenever he hurt himself it would take weeks and weeks before it would finally heal up properly. We spent many days visiting hospitals and doctors surgeries for his wound care to be undertaken and they all marvelled at how this lovely old gentleman could sustain such injury and remain so composed and brave whilst they cleaned and tended to him. As a result, he had many scars on his arms and legs and also on his head. He also had a few bouts of skin cancer on his hand, in his eye, on his head and ear which required surgery which were the result of his many years walking the streets in the sun while doing his totting rounds.

I can remember taking Dad to hospital after one such fall as he had passed out in the hallway at home and when he came around again he realised that he should call me at work. This was 2011 - he was aged 94. When the paramedics took us to hospital we waited in the cubicle to be seen by a doctor. Eventually a young doctor came in quickly firing questions at him - what happened, did he remember falling, did he pass out. Dad was obviously in shock so I answered the doctors questions. I explained that Dad was very independent and for 94 years of age he had kept himself in pretty good shape. The doctor then proceeded to tidy up the wounds, roughly swabbing the cuts (which were pretty big and very ragged) and cutting away excess bits of skin that he felt would hinder healing. Dad sat there grimacing but not making a sound and I could not stand it any longer. I said to the doctor "it's a good job my Dad was a brave soldier in the war because he knows how to deal with pain". The doctor then realised that due to his busy, hectic schedule in A&E he was probably treating my Dad in a rushed and slightly unsympathetic way. He quickly changed his patient manner!

In 2013 I seized the opportunity of taking redundancy and early retirement after working 31 years for Wandsworth Council. I had just sold my house and we had downsized to a lovely bungalow which Dad absolutely loved. I was fortunate to be able to spend the next 3 years at home looking after my Dad as by now he was becoming more frail and having more accidents.

It was in December 2014 that he had his first stroke which left him with some paralysis in his left leg and hand. As soon as he came home from hospital he immediately started all the exercises the hospital had shown him. He was determined to get better and not let the stroke beat him. Early one morning, around 5.30am, I heard some strange noises, huffing and puffing sounds. When I went into his bedroom there he was holding onto the windowsill, determinedly doing his physio exercises. He asked me to video him so that I could put it onto Facebook and his grandchildren both here in the UK and in the USA could see how hard he was working to get himself better. And he did!

When we visited the hospital in January 2015 for his one month follow up, the consultant examined him and explained that Dad had suffered a further bad bleed in his brain but the consultant was astounded that Dad had made such a fantastic recovery. As we left the room the consultant said to Dad "Mr Gurney, I wish all my patients could be like you!". This made Dad very proud of what he had achieved.

During 2015 Dad enjoyed life again. He loved his family and friends visiting him, relishing in being surrounded by his many grandchildren, great and great-great grandchildren along with his nieces and nephews. Dad just loved his family so much and he felt he had a responsibility as one of the only surviving members of his family to be able to answer their questions or seek his advice. Many times a friend or family member would ask a question about Battersea from the old days and my Dad's amazing memory astounded everyone with his recall for people, places and events etc.

Our last holiday together was in August 2015 where we went to the Isle of Sheppey in Kent and stayed in a caravan (Dad did not want the dog to go into kennels so we took our little Mollie with us). My children and their families also came and stayed in caravans so we had a really lovely family holiday. My son and my son in laws took him fishing for the day where he proudly caught more fish than them. It rained all day and as the fish were not biting my Dad looked up to the sky and said "come on Dad, help me catch some fish". That was it, from then on he caught some nice big fish and the guys said that when they took a photo of him with it on his lap he was stroking it and holding it like it was a puppy and they were so worried it was going to expire they quickly took the photo and put it back into the water! My Dad did not let them live it down that he caught the first fish and most of his fish were bigger than theirs. This was one of my Dad's happiest days in a long time as it reminded him of fishing down the Medway in Kent during his earlier years.

It was just before Christmas 2015 that I woke up one morning and found my dear Dad on the living room floor. He could not speak, could not move himself and was freezing cold. I have no idea how long he had lain there, unable to call me to help him. An ambulance was called and we quickly arrived at Epsom General Hospital and Dad was admitted to a ward after they discovered he had suffered a bleed on the brain. After further scans, the doctor came to see him and advised that they were going to send the scans to a neurological surgeon at St George's Hospital to see whether they would operate. Dad agreed that he wanted the surgery as he wanted to recover from this latest illness - he had a goal of reaching his 100th birthday the following year. The doctor eventually came back and said that the neurological surgeon at St George's had refused to undertake the surgery, most likely due to Dad's age. My Dad was extremely disappointed and felt that the doctors should have given him a chance - he said if God wanted him to survive then he would. This was strange to hear my Dad say this because he had held no real religious views and suddenly he was placing his faith in God. However, the answer remained No and for the next few days they concentrated on getting him well enough to come home with me.

On around the 4th day I was sitting with Dad during visiting time and suddenly he wanted to get out of the bed. I got up and walked round to where he was standing and although I was talking to him, asking him where he wanted to go, he was unable to answer me and was shuffling and then he went rigid. I managed to lay him sideways on the bed and shouted for help - he was having his first epileptic seizure. This was a very frightening experience for me, to see my lovely Dad so helpless and I thought he was actually going to die. The staff crowded around him and they confirmed that it was a fit. Once Dad came around they explained to him what they thought it was, arranged for further tests but started him on epilepsy medication. Dad started to improve over the next few days but they had detected further bleeds on his brain. Finally Dad was able to come home and a long process commenced with arranging some assistance at home to help me care for him.

He was discharged home on the 20th December and as soon as he was home he was back on his exercises, determined to get himself well again. He reluctantly accepted that he would have to have carers in twice a day to help him with showering and personal needs and we settled into a new daily routine. He said he only accepted the carers because it would mean that his daughter (me) would not have to attend to his personal needs as it would be too embarrassing for both himself and for me. We settled into a new routine of carers in and out of our house, Dad wearing an alarm bracelet for when I had to leave the house for shopping etc and lots of visitors who wanted to wish him well again. Life was hectic and busy for us both but I was just so happy and relieved to have my wonderful Daddy back home with me again. Our happiness was to be short lived as on the 12th February 2016 he was to suffer a further bleed on his brain - I found him collapsed on the floor again and we once again found ourselves back at Epsom Hospital.

Once again, the surgeons decided against surgery for him. He was so disappointed again and said he would rather be at home than in hospital. He came home and we started our routine again but this time it was with him being much more frail, prone to falling easily and he started to have problems with his chest, coughing and congestion. He was diagnosed with pneumonia and started the first of what was to be 6 different rounds of antibiotics to fight it off. On the 31st March 2016 Dad received a wonderful surprise. His granddaughter, Marti, travelled from Seattle to come and spend a week with him, bringing love and get well hugs from his darling daughter Patsy, his grandchildren Patricia, Susan, Peter and Maria along with the love from his great and great-great grandchildren. He was just so happy, his little face did not stop smiling and he talked non-stop, recalling all the memories of his life and sharing them with Marti to ensure she would take them back to share with everyone over the pond. It was a magical time. We had a baking lesson in our living room with Dad wrapped up in a blanket in his armchair and Marti taking instructions from him on how to make the perfect apple pie. I acted as kitchen assistant, getting all the ingredients ready and bringing them to Marti as she mixed the pastry, rolled it out and lined the baking dish. Dad advised her of every step to take and the end result was a beautiful, very tasty apple pie and Dad marked her 10/10! A wonderful memory for Marti to take back over the pond with her.

Marti left on the 7th April to go back home to her family. It was a very tearful farewell as Marti knew that she would never see her dearest grandfather again. I wasn't thinking along those lines, although my heart was fearful as he was just so unwell. Over the next two weeks the antibiotics failed to treat the pneumonia and the Matron who was coming in each day to see Dad suggested that he go into the cottage hospital for a few days so that he could rest and they could see whether there were any different combinations of antibiotics that would help him. Dad reluctantly agreed to this and so we took him into a lovely little cottage hospital in Epsom.

He soon settled himself into the hospital routine, chatting to everyone he had eye contact with and spreading his sense of humour to all. The setting for this hospital was beautiful, with birds and rabbits outside in the grounds. The doctor examined him and said that she would ask the pharmacy staff whether there were any other drugs they could suggest that would deal with the pneumonia. She met with myself and Dad and explained that there was not much else they could do for him, apart from try to treat the pneumonia and what did he want to do about resuscitation in the event of his heart stopping. She added that she did not think it would be in his best interests to do this. Dad told her strongly that he wanted it done and that it was up to God - if he wanted to take him he would, if he didn't he wouldn't. Even through the seriousness of the situation I was so very proud of my strong, determined Battersea boy! The second day the physiotherapist came to see Dad and put him through his paces on the bed. She then asked him to use the walking frame to walk down the hall and back. Dad took off like a racehorse with the frame and within a minute had walked down the hall and back to his bed. She was astounded - she said she had never met a patient of 99 who had such strength and determination. It was left that she would work with him from the next day to get him more stable and mobile.

The next day Dad started to suffer seizures as they had taken him off the epilepsy medication to start a new course of combined antibiotics. Over the next couple of days Dad continued to deteriorate but the last thing he said was that he wanted to go home. So staff started to put things in place for transport to be booked so that he could do that. Over the weekend he lost consciousness and we were desperately talking to him, telling him that the transport would be coming and we were taking him home. On the Monday morning the ambulance turned up. It was chaotic trying to get everything ready but before I knew it I was sitting in the back of the ambulance with him, telling him every step of the way what part of the route home we were at. When the ambulance crew brought him through the hallway of our bungalow my dear Dad opened his eyes and we could see that he knew where he was - he was finally home.

Dad passed away peacefully on the Wednesday evening, in his own bed with my son Jamie and I holding his hands, telling him we loved him. The last words I said to my darling Daddy were "go and find Mummy and Paula Daddy, they are waiting for you". The greatest man I've ever known had gone on his final journey to join his beloved Rose and daughter Paula. He really was going home.

Printed in Great Britain
by Amazon